Praise from Readers for Internet Marketing Made Easy

"This is a tactical book by an expert tactician. Edmondson's strategies go beyond the 'pop' approach to Internet marketing and reveals strategies that not only work, but they are efficient and cost effective as well."

- Dr. John Mayer, author of *Shadow Warrior: A Thriller*

Brian has the most clear, unintimidating style of teaching I've ever encountered, and I've encountered a lot of so called internet marketing gurus. This book will only take you about an hour to read and will give you lots of actionable steps to take to grow your online business. If you take Brian's easy to follow advice, you will most definitely increase your site's traffic and sales exponentially.

- Aviva Goldfarb, founder of TheScramble.com

Brian is great at making internet marketing easy. I am new to internet marketing and having something like this is invaluable to me to learn what I need to know to have a successful internet marketing strategy and execution process. I highly recommend this book to anyone starting a new business, or moving a current business online.

- Katie Schmatz, author of *7 Secrets to Success I Learned From My Bike*

This book is aimed at the novice, but even seasoned veterans are sure to pick up at least one tip that will flood their funnels with free traffic (I can attest to this because Brian did give me a few of them prior to the book release and they work!).

- Mike Caruana, Santa Monica, CA

Brain is someone that teaches not only the fundamentals of Internet Marketing, but the advanced tips, tricks and strategies that deca-millionaires use to run their businesses. I highly suggest you get this book. You'll love it and use it.

- Cory Boatright, Shortsaleology.com

Internet Marketing Made Easy

The Business Owner's Guide to Getting More Traffic and Making More Money

Brian T. Edmondson

Disclaimer and/or Legal Notices

No express or implied guarantees or warranties have been made or are made by the publisher or author regarding certain incomes, earnings, profits, or other financial claims. Individual results vary, in large part, due to individual circumstances, activity, capability, as well as varying local and global market conditions and other factors.

No responsibility or liability is assumed by the publisher or author for any injury, damage or financial loss sustained to persons or property from the use of this information, personal or otherwise, either directly or indirectly. While every effort has been made to ensure reliability and accuracy of the information within, all liability, negligence or otherwise, from any use, misuse or abuse of the operation of any methods, strategies, instructions or ideas contained in the material herein, is the sole responsibility of the reader

All information is generalized, presented for informational purposes only, and presented "as is" without warranty or guarantee of any kind. This publication is designed to provide accurate and authoritative information in regard to the subject matter covered. It is sold with the understanding that neither the publisher nor author is engaged in rendering legal, accounting or other professional services. If legal advice or other professional assistance is required, the services of a competent professional person should be sought.

Some of the links, if any, mentioned in the publication may be affiliate links and the author and/or publisher may be compensated for recommending those products. However, they will never recommend products that they don't believe in and always welcome questions and feedback regarding all material discussed herein.

Dedication

This book is dedicated to

"The Internet".

Thank you for providing the most powerful vehicle in the history of business.

Contents

Introduction

From the Desk of Brian T. Edmondson

On behalf of myself, and everyone here at the *InternetIncomeCoach.com* team, I'd like to personally thank you for investing in ***Internet Marketing Made Easy: The Business Owner's Guide to Getting More Traffic and Making More Money***.

I truly believe that the Internet, when properly used and understood, is the most powerful tool available in the history of business; and that the opportunity it presents to all of us is unprecedented.

Whether you already have an existing business that is thriving, are looking start a new business venture, or just want to make a few extra dollars by turning your passions into profits, there is something here for you.

If this is your first time coming across me and my company, Internet Income Coach, then I'd like to personally welcome you to our community of successful online entrepreneurs.

Sincerely,

Brian T. Edmondson

InternetIncomeCoach.com

P.S. I'd like to invite you to download a free copy of your ***Internet Profit Report (a $47 value free).*** As an added bonus you'll also get a free subscription to my email only newsletter where I reveal my latest tips, tricks, and online marketing discoveries. You can do that right now at:

http://www.InternetIncomeCoach.com

Chapter 1

Spreading Your Expertise to a Global Audience

The Internet isn't just a place where friends gather on Facebook to share pictures of their vacations and catch up with old school friends.

It's become a platform for men and women of every age to share their passions and expertise with others – and make a profit from it.

Whether you're a professional who already has a reputation offline, or a hobbyist who has a knack for something specific, the Internet can help you reach more people, guide them with their needs, and get paid for it.

There are many professionals and experts working in local businesses who are just now discovering the potential that the Internet gives them to expand their reach.

It doesn't matter if you're a coach, consultant, author or other expert in your field - you're going to be amazed at the vast opportunity you're about to unearth – and how easy it is to master it.

Hobbyists also love how the Internet gives them a way to connect with others passionate about their topic, and you'll be pleased to know that people will pay for guidance on reaching the same level that you're at!

It's Time to Increase Your Exposure to Potential Customers

If you're a local entrepreneur or business professional, there are many costs that prohibit you from achieving your financial goals more quickly. In order to grab the attention of the right audience, you have to invest in offline advertising, which can be costly and may not always be very effective.

If you have a hobby, you may or may not have a group of like-minded people to interact with – and even if you do, they might not have a need for guidance as a beginner.

Once you learn how to use the Internet from a branding and business building perspective, which I'm going to teach you in this book, you'll realize that the online exposure you'll get delivers a never-ending stream of prospective customers with a much lower investment than what the offline world requires (and in many cases - free).

The first thing you have to do is put away any fear or intimidation about creating a presence online that brands you as an expert. Everyone is an expert if it means there's someone else out there looking up to you for advice and insight – even if you're only one step ahead of them.

Many people feel confident offline, but as soon as they begin thinking about a global reach, it makes them second-guess their expertise. Once you understand what people want and how to provide it to them, you'll have all your fears dismissed.

You don't want to have the mindset of "someday" haunting you. There's no reason to wait until *you* feel like you're "good enough" to be branding yourself as an expert online.

Expanding Your Reach Provides More Personal Satisfaction

Have you ever helped guide a client or customer – or even a friend – into improving their life in some way, overcoming a challenge, or even learning a new skill?

If so, you'll understand how personally rewarding that feeling is – when they thank you repeatedly and tell you how grateful they are for how much you shared with them.

Imagine that feeling multiplied over and over again.

Once you expand your presence from a small offline world to an endless online global marketplace, you'll be in awe of the treasures you'll get in terms of personal satisfaction.

As a professional, you know there are people out there who need your help. You can go online and begin changing lives. Maybe you're a life coach who helps men and women go from a state of perpetual depression and hopelessness to a place where they wake up each day consumed by happiness!

Or perhaps you are an avid knitter who is always helping people learn the ropes. You could create an online business presence where not only would people appreciate your tutorials, but they would pay you for them!

You might be thinking that your expertise or hobby isn't something anyone would pay for. In most instances, you'd be wrong.

Consumers go online looking for information quickly. They're not looking for the household name or the Fortune 500 companies. They want to learn from a real person who was once in their position or who understands where they're coming from.

If a person desperate for some motivation buys a book from Tony Robbins, chances are they're never going to interact with him personally. But if you had a book online or a membership site, perhaps – then there's a good chance they might be able to ask questions, get feedback, and express their thanks to you for a job well done.

Building a connection with your audience is truly rewarding. You may not be seeing these people in person, but that doesn't mean you won't be forming real relationships with what rapidly becomes your loyal fan base.

The Internet Is Easy to Master With the Right Guidance

You might be able to envision the possibilities to some degree, but the thought of creating an online presence still feels overwhelming to you.

The good news is – while you may be starting from scratch today, it won't take you long to understand how it all works – and you'll be able to create your own home on the 'net with ease.

Unlike an offline office, a web-based business enjoys low overhead and almost no start-up costs. I'm going to show you how you can easily create your own website where clients and fellow enthusiasts can find you, buy products from you, and send other people your way.

It's easy to suffer from what's known as "information overload" when you're a newbie to the online business world.

As long as you slow down and make a plan for your profitable venture online, you'll be headed in the right direction.

The learning curve is relatively short. There aren't a lot of technical tasks to understand. It's more about strategy and building a buzz – something anyone can do once they see how it all works.

What's wonderful about this approach is that you can automate many parts of your business, like selling products, and focus your efforts on what you truly enjoy – changing lives for the better.

That might mean teaching people a craft, coaching them to make different decisions, or informing them about something they need to know. Information products sell very well online, and there's no reason why you shouldn't be poised to leverage your knowledge in a profitable way.

Chapter 2

Your Audience Is Looking for You Right Now

In order to understand the possibilities, you need to get a clear understanding about how experts connect with their potential customers online.

How Search Engines and Social Sharing Bring People Together

Whenever you want to look up something online, chances are you fire up the computer, pull up your favorite browser (like FireFox, Internet Explorer, Chrome, or Safari) and then go to the search engine of your choice (perhaps Google or Bing).

You type something into the search engine and see what results come up for you. Maybe you're looking for a recipe for peach cobbler or a health tip on how to get rid of a headache naturally.

Google (or whatever search engine you're on) has created a behind the scenes formula called an algorithm that calculates which websites and pages on those websites would best serve your needs.

They're not always 100% accurate, but there's a fairly good chance that you're going to find the information you're looking for quickly.

Now – put yourself on the other side of that equation.

You're an expert who maybe wants to teach people how to cure a headache without medicines. Maybe you teach a variety of stress relief options like guided imagery, meditation, or self-hypnosis.

You want to be one of those top websites that Google delivers to the person who is awake at 2 AM with a pounding headache.

You want the person using that search engine to click on **your link**, land on **your blog or website**, and bookmark it because they find you to be such a **valuable resource.**

Maybe you have an online short report to give to them about how to cure headaches with natural herbs and holistic treatments. They see a little box asking them to sign up for that free report, and get a subscription to your site using their name and email address, so they fill it out.

Now you have the ability to contact *them*, not just wait for them to come back to your site.

Over time, you share good tips with that person via email (an automated email that goes out to everyone on your list), and they begin to trust you and look forward to your insight.

They buy products that you sell – things that you created. They buy things that you recommend that are created by others (things you get a commission on).

Now let's take the hobbyist into consideration. Let's say that you love to play golf! You have some great tips on stopping a slice or maybe intentionally slicing the ball to pull off a difficult shot.

Your online blog shares your passion for golf and all of the gadgets golfers' love – from the handheld GPS systems to the best balls made for staying in the fairway.

What you share on your site tells Google that you're a great resource for other people who love golf. You see, Google's not looking for a degree or a certain number of years in experience.

They're looking for what real consumers want – good information. Good sharing. Good interaction with your readers.

So they rank your site high and begin sending people to your website. There, you have an email subscription box where you promise to share more great tips. Along comes John Doe.

He's gone to Google and typed in the phrase, "how to fix a golf slice" because this Saturday, he's playing in a local foursome tournament and he does not want to be throwing his clubs into the pond on the third hole.

You happen to have a blog post with that exact same title. He clicks through to your site. He sees a free report you're giving away when people subscribe to your email list that's all about fixing a slice. He signs up.

In the follow up emails that you send him, not only does he get to hear your advice about slices, but you've recommended the SKLZ Rick Smith Slice Eliminator - Swing Path Trainer.

It sells for around $32 on Amazon.com and because you used a link known as an affiliate link, you get a commission whenever John buys it from you.

Whether you're an established professional offline or just someone who has a passion for something, the Internet is where search engines are going to play the middleman that brings you together with people who are eager to hear what you have to say – and willing to pay money for it.

Take a Look at Keywords in Your Niche

A niche is your area of expertise. You can have a broad niche like "self-help" or a narrower niche like "self-help for anxiety."

You just learned about how a potential paying customer uses a search engine to find your website. I want to show you how website owners and experts just like you use keywords to attract search engine traffic.

A keyword is a single word or phrase that someone uses online to find the information they need.

Broad keywords are usually single words like "golf" or "health" – they're very broad and aren't very helpful in narrowing down the results when you use them on sites like Google.

Long-tail keywords are typically what your audience will use to find your site and figure out who has the right expertise. It's a longer string of words that turns into a specific phrase.

Let's take life coaches as our example here. You're a life coach who wants to use the Internet to sell your own eBooks (or print books) and get more clients who pay you to coach them on the phone or through a tool like Skype where you can video chat.

You wouldn't just try to rank high on Google for a broad keyword like "life coach" because that might include all of the people who want to learn how to become a certified life coach – and they're not your target audience.

You want to learn how to rank your site for keyword phrases like this:

- Where to find a life coach (368,000 people searching for this each month)
- Life coach for women (1,300 people searching for this each month)
- Life coach for hire (480 people searching for this each month)
- Life coach for teenagers (260 people searching for this each month)

When you make a plan to expand your reach to an online audience, keywords and phrases will play an important role. First you have to know how to find them, and then where and how to use them.

Tools are available to help you do your keyword research. They come in free and paid versions. Some are really easy to use, and others more complex.

What you generally do is start out broad and dig down into the process of gathering your long-tail keyword phrases.

Google provides a free keyword tool online that anyone can use. So you would start by entering your broad niche word or phrase. Let's return to our knitting niche for a moment.

You would enter the word "knit" and see what shows up. Here, I would discover that people want to know about:

- Free knitting patterns
- Knitting for beginners
- How to knit a scarf (a wonderful topic you could write a report on to get people to sign up to your email list)
- Knitting needles (a great affiliate commission phrase where you could recommend some)

You would be compiling all of these keywords in a file somewhere on your computer. You can use a Word processor or an Excel spreadsheet if you want – whatever you're comfortable with.

Then you want to start digging deeper. Let's take the phrase "knitting needles." When you type that into a keyword tool, you then find out that people want to know about:

- Interchangeable knitting needles
- Bamboo knitting needles
- Addi turbo knitting needles
- 5 mm knitting needles
- Wooden knitting needles
- Double pointed knitting needles

And you keep on digging down until you have a hearty list of keywords and phrases that you're going to use online to attract the people who want to learn from you. You might find phrases like "circular bamboo knitting needles" and then "circular bamboo knitting needle sets" and so on.

Don't get overwhelmed by the volume of keywords that you find in your niche. It's good to have a long list of topics that people are searching for so that you can cater to their needs with the information you share with them.

It's Not Just About Information – It's About Presentation

So you might be thinking (after researching a bunch of keywords in your niche) that all you'll have to do is use those words on your website and Google will reward you with lots of traffic to your site.

That's not quite how it works.

Keywords are important – there's no doubt about that – but once you get someone to your site, it's how you convey the information that you want to share that matters most.

Your own personal style is what can't be replicated by anyone else. There's a target audience for everyone in a niche. You can enjoy the fact that with a global audience, you'll be able to find a large group of individuals who appreciate what you have to say and *how* you say it.

Maybe you're nurturing and take a "hand holding" approach. Perhaps you're motivating with a tough love slant. There's an audience for everyone on the spectrum.

At the same time, you want to realize that there will always be a group of people who aren't cut out to be your target audience. There's no way to make sure that everyone likes you at all times.

So you might find as you start expanding your reach online that you're more aware of who is attracted to your message and style and who leaves because you're not a good fit for them.

Don't let it hurt your feelings. Your expertise and passion is going to become profitable online because you're a magnet for like-minded people.

Maybe you discover that you like to write long blog posts, or make videos for your blog. Some people will be in the "can't get enough" category, while others will be turned off by video or long blog posts.

Don't worry about how much competition there is in a niche or for the keywords you want to rank well for. Just concentrate on how to leverage your own personal style and you'll enjoy the results you get from your efforts.

Chapter 3

Creating Your Home on the Internet

Once you feel comfortable with the idea of expanding your reach to the online community, you'll want to create a home for your message – a place where your audience can gather to learn from you, buy products or service from you, and refer others to you.

There are basically six elements to a website that I feel are important for you to know. One of them we'll go into detail about in the next chapter. You'll start with the process of buying a domain and hosting account, make a decision about what type of site you want, and then add some elements that help you increase the communication with your audience.

Selecting a Domain for Your Site

You've learned a bit about keywords and how they can attract your audience to your offerings online.

The very first place you'll want to put that to use is in the selection of your domain – but it's not a cut and dry selection.

There are three ways you can choose a good domain name. The first is to brand yourself with your own name online. So if you were Jane Doe, you could register janedoe.com.

The second method is to use a keyword phrase in your domain. Let's pull an example from earlier using the knitting niche. You might use a domain like howtoknit.com – which reflects that it's a beginner's knitting website.

Or, you can do a combination of the two. That would be something like this: JaneDoeCoaching.com or JaneDoeKnitting.com. Using this method, you're using two-pronged approach by including your brand name and your niche topic.

There are some things you need to keep in mind when you're choosing a good domain.

Shorter domain names are better than longer ones. The more you expect your audience to remember, the higher the chance they'll get it wrong. So you wouldn't want to choose a domain like this:

JaneDoesCourseOnHowToKnitScarvesQuickly.com

Another tip is to always try to get your ".com" domain. It's okay to have a ".net" or ".org", or even a ".info", but everyone typically types ".com" after a domain name, so you want to shoot for that.

Many people will register all of the domains: .com, .org, .net, etc. This is a good idea, but not necessary at first. You may want to eventually grab them just to prevent competitors from trying to build a site there and siphon off some of your traffic.

A domain name is going to cost you around $10 to $15 depending on where you register it.

Whenever you order your domain from a site like GoDaddy, they're going to try to add on a million extras before you get to the checkout page. You don't need all of the bells and whistles like site building tools and extra security. Just the domain, that's it.

I personally purchase all of my domain names at NameCheap. They're a great low cost domain name registrar; and their corporate culture is one that supports free speech and free commerce online. You can learn more about them at:

InternetIncomeCoach.com/namecheap

Choosing a Good Hosting Account

Hosting is what will take your site live – and keep it live for when visitors land on it. So choosing a hosting company with a good record of "up time" (meaning the sites don't go down a lot) is important.

HostGator is a good hosting company that has a proven track record with up time. They boast an impressive rate among competitors. But you want to look for other important elements in a hosting company, too.

First, customer service is vital to your site's success. You want to make sure that you can call anytime – 24 hours a day, 7 days a week, 365 days a year – because that's how often your business will be accessed online.

Some companies (and HostGator is one) will be available by email, phone or live chat whenever you need help. You want to find a company whose representatives are friendly and knowledgeable.

Another thing you want your hosting company to do is have many built in features. For example, it might have site building tools built in (so you don't need the ones your domain registrar tries to sell you), it has a blog installer built in, and statistics tools that help you analyze how your site is doing online.

Of course price is a factor, too. Hosting shouldn't cost an arm and a leg. You should be able to pay around $10 to $15 a month or less for unlimited domains. Most hosting companies will give steep discounts when you order a longer plan, too – like a year's worth of hosting paid up front.

As I mentioned already, I host most of my websites with HostGator. If you choose to host with them I would recommend going with their "baby" plan which allows you to host an unlimited number of domains under one account.

If you use coupon code "**incomecoach25**" you can save an additional 25% off your hosting account order.

You can learn more about HostGator's hosting plans at:

InternetIncomeCoach.com/hostgator

Some Experts Use Static Websites

A static website is something that doesn't have a lot of interactive features. It's not a blog where you have daily or weekly posts and the ability to interact with your audience.

You can certainly go the static website route if you want to – especially if you have dozens and dozens of products that you want to create pages for separately.

A static website for a professional would possibly have the following pages:

Home page that greets your visitors and gives a brief overview about their problem and the solution you provide.

- Services page that shows the various services you provide.
- Products page that acts like a catalog to show off your products.
- Specials page that gives discount coupons for Internet customers.

- Contact page that allows people to get in touch if they have questions.

These aren't set in stone – you could have any pages you like on your static website.

Simple Steps to Create a Blog on Your Site

A blog is such a wonderful tool to help you increase your brand exposure online. Search engines love blogs because they provide fresh content. A static site is often created and forgotten about, but a blog has on-going content to serve the needs of an audience.

With the push of a button and a few details added in, you can easily install a blog on your site and begin blogging about your expertise in an instant!

Once a blog is installed, you will log in to what's known as your blog's dashboard. That's where the behind-the-scenes settings are initiated by you. Basically, all you're doing is deciding how you want your blog to run.

For example, you can give your blog a title, create pages or blog posts and publish them instantly or schedule them for a future time.

You can choose a layout for your blog that appeals to you. This is what's known as a blog theme.

There are literally thousands of free and paid themes and templates out there. I usually recommend going with a paid theme as they offer more features and are periodically updated.

You can find some of my preferred theme and template providers in the Resources section at the end of this book.

Learn How to Use Effective Squeeze Pages

A squeeze page is a very simple page that you can use on your website to help you build a subscriber list of people who are interested in your message or what you have to sell.

It's a small page that generally includes one or two headlines, a few bullet points, and what's known as an opt-in form, where they can enter their first name and an email so you can stay in touch with them via follow up emails. This is something we'll talk about in detail in Chapter 6.

A squeeze page can be simple text or include a video component. Some experts feel it helps them build their list if they use a combination of the two media formats, since video helps build trust.

One mistake many experts make on their squeeze pages when they first set up a website with a squeeze page is that they have too much going on in the page itself.

A squeeze page is meant to "squeeze" the name and email address out of the visitors. So you don't want to have a myriad of options available for them. You want them to sign up, or click out.

If you have links to all of your products, your YouTube account, and so on, then you miss out on the opportunity to communicate with them again once they leave.

Another mistake people make is in putting too much information on their squeeze page. All you want to do is convey what they're going to get with 1-2 headlines and a few short bullet points.

Remember, if they sign up to your list, you'll have time to contact them and inform them better about your expertise. Don't feel like you have to flood them with information right now.

Should Your Site Have a Forum?

Some experts hunger for a place they can build a community online – somewhere you might be able to send your offline clients to, as well as attract an online audience.

Forums can sometimes achieve this goal for you, but there are some drawbacks to running a forum on your site as well, so we need to analyze whether or not it's best for you.

A forum is certainly easy to install. Like a blog, it's another push button addition and suddenly, it's live! That's definitely a positive point to make about forums.

But once it's live, you have to realize that this is like a garden – it has to be tended to or else unsavory characters will invade it and overpower what you originally hoped it would be.

You'll either need to run the forum yourself (and that means checking to see if you have time for this) or get help with it. Sometimes participants on a forum will volunteer to be moderators, and those are the people who will keep spammers and antagonistic people out.

A forum does help you build a community. It's a great way to spread information. But you might want to put that detail on your blog instead.

If you do decide to go with a forum, then you might consider making it a paid feature of your site. This keeps out the riff-raff and allows you to profit from the time that you put into it.

Another option, if you're looking to get more community involvement, is to set up a Facebook Group in conjunction with your website.

Making a website sounds like a harrowing task, but once you go through it step-by-step, you'll realize it's not so intimidating. There's plenty of help available and you should have no trouble getting your site off the ground in a single day!

Chapter 4

High Tech Meets High Touch

In the last chapter we touched on what it meant to have a blog as a professional or enthusiast who wants increased branding and exposure online and to turn that into profits.

Many people go online to learn about blogging and think there's nothing to it other than slapping up some articles onto the web. But the goal of your content is to attract an audience that will take action on your site – sign up to your list, buy your products or services, and engage with you.

So you need more than just delivery of some keyword-rich articles. I want to show you the best way to build a formidable blog audience by telling you what it is that they want from you.

Blog Readers Crave Personality

There's nothing worse than landing on a site for information and not feeling like you can trust it because you aren't sure who's behind it.

Some experts, authors and coaches feel confident in their careers, but lack the same confidence to put themselves out there online. You'll need to showcase your personality in order to gain trust with your visitors.

It's not the same as having an offline client who sits in your office and gets to see your mannerisms and hear your voice. Those people automatically build a deeper connection with you.

Online, it's a combination of text and graphics working toward building your relationship with your visitor, so you have to be transparent with your message.

A personality is something everyone has – but many online experts have trouble showing. It might feel a bit intimidating or embarrassing to share your thoughts – but look at an expert like Tony Robbins (or even Oprah Winfrey).

What endears those professionals to the masses isn't just the information that they share.

It's the fact that we get to hear about their background, their struggles, their triumphs and innermost thoughts.

You don't always have to tell a personal tale to make a connection, either. Just being able to share your opinions on things can help others figure out if they feel compatible with you.

Don't be afraid to be nurturing, motivational, or even a firecracker if that's the way you help people get the solutions they need in their lives! There will be an audience for you who needs exactly what you're offering – *exactly* the way you're offering it.

Being Relevant Is Key

When someone lands on your website or blog, they want to know that the content and advice they're going to hear will be what you said it would be about.

If they go to a search engine and type in "healthy cooking" and they see a site come up that says "Healthy Cooking Magazine – Recipes, Low-Fat," but then they land there and find healthy *dog* meals, then that's a little misleading. That site would need to clarify that the healthy meals were for pets, not humans.

When you set up your site and blog, there will be a place in the settings that lets you place what's known as a "tag line."

A tag line is a motto of sorts. It tells search engines (and humans who are considering clicking on your link) what your site is all about.

So for example, you might be a cooking enthusiast. You could have a domain called CookingWithShannon.com but it doesn't narrow down to the visitor what kind of cooking you'll be doing.

A tag line can help. It might say, "Learn to Cook Healthy Meals for Your Family," or "Cooking Tips to Help You Say Goodbye to the Microwave." Both tag lines help you understand a bit more about what the site is.

Some experts go a little too broad in their online efforts. They know they want an online presence, but they think, "Well, I'll buy one domain and stick everything on there – my books, services, vacation pictures, etc."

A professional profitable blog will have a good focus – it won't be a catch all for every topic you have an inkling to write about for the day. For example, if it's a website about your fiction books because you're an author, then you wouldn't blog about baby strollers or home repair tips.

One reason you want to be relevant for what your readers want is because sites have what's known as a "bounce rate." A bounce is when someone leaves your site after only viewing the page that they land on.

You want visitors to stay and look around and spend time on your blog. Search engines love to see these types of sites and give them credibility as authority sites.

A high bounce rate means they're sending visitors to you and you're not satisfying them, so it makes the search engine rethink their decision to showcase your domain as a result whenever someone comes to them.

You'll be able to find the statistics for your site's performance once you have it live by using free tools like Google Analytics. They'll tell you how visitors are interacting on your site so that you can make improvements that attract more people – and keep them there.

Share Your Best Stuff – Free

Bloggers have to be willing to share good information for free. Some experts mistakenly think that they have to sell every single bit of information, but that doesn't give your prospective audience a reason to trust you.

Here are some basic ideas of the types of blog posts you can create – and these are just the tip of the iceberg:

Favorite ideas

Because you're the expert, your audience wants to know what *you* like best. If you're an author, you might share your favorite author that *you* read. Or the best writing book (since you know fellow writers will be tuning into your success).

If you're a life coach, then you might blog about your favorite way to confront a difficult decision, or the best way you know to de-stress after a particularly hectic day.

A knitting professional could blog about their favorite type of yarn, the best pattern that you personally enjoy knitting, or your own preference for the type of knitting needle you use.

Numbered tip lists

Numbered tip lists go over extremely well with a blog audience. You could do something like this: 7 Reasons Why...Top 10 List of... 101 Ways to...4 Steps to a...

Those numbered lists can work in any niche.

Curated content

Curated content is when you build your own content based around someone else's content. You're basically pulling in a snippet of information and then adding your own commentary.

You can't confuse this with copying someone else's content – because that's called plagiarism. But you can pull in a short paragraph or a few quotes or a video someone did and credit them for it as you add your own commentary.

Reviews of products...and more

Reviews of products are helpful to your blog audience because you're being a guide in the niche, helping them make good buying decisions. So let's say you have expertise as a holistic health consultant.

You could buy, read and review a book about holistic health – even if you have a book of your own! People often want to learn from multiple resources, not just one.

Or you could review a tangible product like crystals or healing stones that they can buy on Amazon. Don't just tell people what you think they want to hear – give them your honest evaluation of what the products are like.

A Certain Level of Frequency

Blogs need to be cultivated for growth. The more you blog, the more frequently search engines send what's known as "bots" or "spiders" to your site to see what's new.

They're looking to index each page and post in their files so that whenever someone types a keyword or phrase into their search tool, they can go into their files and retrieve the best sites – which you hope to be a part of.

The best blog frequency is daily, of course. But you don't have to commit to that kind of rigorous schedule.

Some blogging experts post more than one blog entry per day, while others post a weekly blog. You can schedule your blogs to post in the future if you want to spend a block of time writing them and let them drip out to your readers over time.

One great way to use your expertise on your new blog is to create an editorial calendar. This lets you know which topics need to be written and which date they need to be posted on.

When you start catering to your audience on a regular, timely basis, they develop a habit of checking in with you. Some might log onto your site each morning with a cup of coffee to see what you have to say that's new each day.

Or maybe you have a video blog every Saturday evening that people tune into. The possibilities are endless. You just have to set a schedule that is right for you – one that is consistent, but won't overwhelm you.

A Community of Like -Minded People

A blog has the best potential to help you expand your reach and make increased profits when you turn it into a community of readers. There are other ways to do it, of course.

You could post your blog and move on each time, never interacting with those who comment (if you even have comments open to the public), never fostering a discussion.

But it's more rewarding when your blog readers get to know one another and are all there as fans and followers of your home on the web. This makes it more inviting to others who stumble on your blog.

If you enable the comments on your blog posts (which you should), then it's important to respond to them and let your readers know they've been heard. Keep in mind that many people feel intimidated commenting on a blog, so you're there to be a good host or hostess and make them feel welcome.

Chapter 5

Developing Your Brand on the Internet

Offline, you might garner the attention of clients and customers by being a specific type of professional – a counselor specializing in addiction, for example. But online, you want to set yourself apart as a brand.

What Do You Want to Be Known For?

You might have gone into your career with a passion to help people have the solutions they need to make life better in some way. You went to college or secured your training, but you may not have considered your brand.

Branding isn't just for big businesses. Online it's especially important because it helps you siphon off sales from the competition. You have to be able to figure out what your brand is all about before you start promoting yourself online.

Branding isn't just about putting yourself out there and making your presence known. It's about really focusing on how you want people to see you. When they think of your name, do you know what one word you'd hope they find synonymous with your brand?

Think about it for a minute.

It should be an adjective that describe how your business operates, like this:

- Author = captivating

- Chef = innovative
- Life coach = inspiring
- Counselor = nurturing
- Plumber = reliable

Carefully think about your branding journey because you don't want to pigeonhole yourself into something too narrow. Remember – you're on the World Wide Web, so you may want to branch out from what you're doing offline and expand on the business.

This might require you to have a broader branding strategy. You'll be working your branding into your online presence in many ways, which we're about to discuss next, so spend a little time thinking about longevity and how you want to be known.

Take Advantage of Guest Blogging Opportunities

Guest blogging is a fantastic way to get more traffic to your own website, increased branding and exposure, and more sales of your products and services online!

There are thousands (if not millions) of blog owners who have so many plates spinning in the air that they can't possibly create enough content for their blog on a regular basis.

So what they do is recruit other professionals in the same niche to stop by and post a blog on their site (which already has established traffic). You, in return, are given a byline and a link back to your own site.

There are a few ways to find guest blogging opportunities.

First, as you become known on the 'net, you'll get emails from other bloggers who approach you and ask if you'd like to provide a guest blog for their website.

You don't want to become a machine who just creates content for other people nonstop. Make sure you have time – and that the site is reputable and has a steady flow of traffic for you to benefit from.

You can also approach some blog owners whose blogs you like and email them asking if they would like you to provide a guest blog post. Sometimes, this will be a reciprocal arrangement where you also let them write a guest blog post for your site.

Before you email them, make sure you convey that you're aware of what their site is all about. Come up with one or more possible guest blog topics that you'd like to do for them – or better yet, have the blog post already written and email it with your byline and link already in place. This allows them to just plug it in and quickly email you with a positive reply.

You can also use Google or other search engines to find blogs that accept guest bloggers. Just type in your niche or professional and the words *guest blog.* So if I type in *psychology guest blog,* I see many opportunities for psychology blogs that have guest bloggers on them. Then you reach out to the blog owner and offer to do a guest post for them.

Use Professional Graphics to Help Brand Your Business

Many professionals who go online to create a website of their own simply use the free graphics that come with their blog theme or website creation tools. But this doesn't help you brand yourself as something original.

You can buy complete website graphics for an affordable price. They can design a whole host of things for you, including:

- A WordPress theme for your blog
- A static website design

- A squeeze page – with or without a frame for your video if you include that media format
- A Twitter background and header if you get into those social websites
- Digital covers for your books if you begin publishing online
- Banner ads
- A logo for your business...and more!

You may not know what all of the elements are that you'll need yet, but a graphic designer will. For example, you can simply look at a package and order a "minisite" and that will come with a header, footer, background, and possibly a few eCovers if you're publishing online.

Unless you are highly skilled at creating graphics, it's always best to outsource this to a professional who is familiar with online graphics (print are not the same, so make sure that whoever you hire is experienced with online media).

For a very modest fee compared to any type of offline business you could have an entire site designed – and it will reflect your niche, include your branding motto if you want it to, and even include your professional picture if you'd like that on there.

The best way to find a good graphics designer is to either get word of mouth recommendations (you can ask in online marketing forums for advice on this). Or, you could post a project on a freelance site like Elance.com and get bids from graphic designers, look at their portfolio, and hire one who makes you feel comfortable. Another site I really like to outsource graphics inexpensively to is Fiverr.com.

Be Available for Interviews

Interviews are a fantastic way to gain extra branding in your niche. There are many ways interviews are done online.

Podcast shows, which are like online radio shows, often interview experts in a particular niche. You can go on sites like BlogTalkRadio.com or others and find shows in your niche. Check to see if they do interviews and then contact them to offer your expertise.

YouTube shows are popular avenues for interviewing experts. These days, you can be interviewed on video chat using a simple free tool like Skype (or Google Hangouts), and the person recording it can do a split screen shot where both yourself and the interviewer are shown on camera.

Look for shows on YouTube that interview experts in your niche. Then contact the person who owns the account and offer your services as someone who can be interviewed.

Text interviews are also popular – they make great blog content. So we already talked about how to contact bloggers about guest blog posts. For interviews, you would do the same thing!

Make sure you also have a page on your website that lets people know how to contact you for an interview or guest blog post.

Use Press Releases Online to Syndicate Branding

Press releases aren't just for major companies to send to a print news desk. They're routinely used online by everyday professionals who want to increase their branding and exposure.

There are hundreds of free and paid press release (PR) companies where you can submit your PR to and it will get listed online, sending links and traffic back to your website.

If you're an author, you can use a press release to announce that your book is released. Inside the release, you can tell what the book is about and provide a quote as the author – or have a fan of the book provide a quote.

You can use a press release to:

- Announce a new book release

- Announce the launch of your website or blog
- Announce any new products or services that you provide
- Announce significant news in your niche

The last option in the list is the one you'll use whenever there's nothing specific happening on your site – no products or services being released. It's an easy way to increase your branding as an expert because whenever there's niche news, people turn to experts for an interpretation of the facts.

It's very easy to find news in your niche. Go to Google and type in the niche and choose "News" from the options Google gives you. So let's say you're a reflexologist.

You go to Google and type in "reflexology" and click News. When I do this, I discover the following possible news stories that you could create a press release and be quoted in it as the expert:

- Reflexology being touted as a treatment for arthritis
- Reflexology being administered to senior citizens in nursing homes

Or if you're a counselor, you might pick up on the myriad of counseling news stories, like the mass shootings and mental health connection. Or comment about the story that discusses how pastors often counsel their congregation, but haven't had professional counseling training.

You'll find a wide array of opportunities for you to create a press release about the story and include your own quote, with a link back to your website.

Keep in mind that a press release is written in the same way you read a print newspaper story. It might help to even look at a print newspaper while you craft your piece.

Aside from the specific quote, everything in the press release should be factual. It should answer the basic questions:

- Who
- What
- When
- Where
- Why
- How

Once you put a press release out there, it can get syndicated by organizations and websites that want to pick it up for content, but your links and byline will stay intact, helping you brand yourself as a go-to expert in your niche!

Chapter 6

Unleashing the Power of Email Marketing

Once you develop a presence online and start generating good content that attracts the right kind of people, you'll want to take advantage of what's known as an opt-in list.

What Is a List?

This is when you have a sign up form on your website or blog where people can enter their name and email address so that you can communicate with them at a later date.

They are opting-in to your list voluntarily, not by force or because you stole their information.

For many people, handing over their name and email address is a very personal situation. They are expecting you to respect this information and protect it – so you never want to sell it to other marketers or treat your list with any disrespect.

Once the names are collected, they'll be in your email marketing database and you'll have the opportunity to send out automated emails that are personalized with their name.

What Will You Give in Exchange?

When someone hands over their personal contact information, they're usually expecting to get something in return. There are two ways you can approach the offer for your opt-in list.

First, you can promise a series of tips sent directly to their email inbox. So for instance, let's say you're in the stress niche. You could offer a 7-part series on how to handle stress naturally.

What will happen is your visitor signs up and gets the first tip immediately, with a series of tips coming to their inbox over the course of 7 days.

Another way you can do it is to offer an immediate downloadable gift. This might be a short report or an eBook that you're giving away in exchange for them allowing you to communicate with them in the future.

As soon as they sign up, a welcome email is sent to them, with a link that lets them download the free gift.

There are three ways you can put a free gift together.

First, you can write it yourself. Or, if you want to send a video or podcast gift, you can record those on your own, too.

Second, you can outsource it to a freelance service provider. When it's ghostwritten, it means you pay for the creation and own the sole rights to the product so you can do anything with it that you wish – and put your name on it.

And last, you can invest in some content known as private label rights (PLR). PLR content is similar to ghostwritten content – but instead of costing $10-30 per page, it only costs $1 per page – because there will be multiple buyers.

There is PLR content for almost any niche. So for example, you could buy a 30 page eBook on Time Management, put your name on it and edit or alter it in any way you see fit, and give that away to the people who sign up to join your list.

It's one of the fastest ways to get a freebie gift for your list. To find it online, do a search on Google for your niche topic and PLR, like this: Diet PLR, Stress PLR eBook, Organic Product PLR, etc.

Technical Setup of Your List

There are many different email autoresponder tools available for you to use. Some are free and some are paid. The free versions are limited in the number of subscribers they allow you to use, plus they often include other advertisements – which you don't want.

One good company to use is Aweber. The first month is just $1 and it's just under $20 a month after that. You can build multiple lists, too. So if you are a life coach, for example, you might have a separate list for all of the following:

- Life coach for women
- Life coach for teenagers
- Life coach for artists
- Life coach for doctors
- Life coach for athletes...and so on

That way all of your email messages could be tailored to that audience. You could approach the athletes differently than you do the teens, etc.

This helps your subscribers because the messages aren't too broad – they feel like they're specifically meant for them.

Setting up your autoresponder is easy and Aweber will literally walk you through each step on your screen.

Once the list is set up, you'll click on the Forms page where you'll choose a template for your opt-in box (it can match the design of your site or blog), the size, and what you want it to say.

For example, you might choose a template that has healthy foods on it if you're a nutritionist. The text might say, "Sign Up for Free Weekly Recipes Delivered Straight to Your Inbox!"

Once you design it in the system, you'll simply take the HTML code it gives you and paste it into your blog or website where you want it. You always want to test it after it's live by signing up to your list yourself so that you can make sure the process is working.

As I mentioned earlier, when it comes to building your list and marketing with email, I highly recommend using Aweber. You can learn more about Aweber and get your first month $1-trial at:

InternetIncomeCoach.com/aweber

Communicating With Your List

There are two different choices of emails that you can create to communicate with your list. The first is called a broadcast email. Broadcasts are sent one time to your list, so anyone who signs up after it's sent will not receive it.

This is perfect if you're running a sale or special, or want to alert your list to an interview you're doing or a webinar (online live seminar) perhaps.

Then there's the follow up email. These are emails you create that drip out to your list on a schedule that you create. Every person who signs up to your list will get this series of emails over time.

Some people send out daily emails, or weekly – but many schedule the contact for every 3 days or so, a good blend for those who need frequent contact versus those who don't want to hear from you every day.

Another thing you can do is set up a specific list for a weekly digest. This way, those who want to scroll down and read all of your week's worth of emails in one sitting can do so.

There's a fine balance between communicating with your list with value and communicating with them just to have your name in front of them. One is beneficial to both you and the prospective customer – and the other is just beneficial to you.

Make sure that when send emails, it's because you have something interesting and valuable to say to your list. It can be small, simple tips – but don't email just to say hi.

You can also use a list to cater to buying customers versus prospective customers. Here's how that works:

Let's say you create an eBook about natural healing. You buy a domain for it and have a little minisite designed for it. You're selling it for $17 and the payments go straight to your PayPal.

A visitor lands on your domain and buys the eBook. They get a download email for the eBook and get to opt-into your list. This list happens to be for buyers only.

Your follow up and future broadcast communications to this list can be different from the ones you send out to people who only downloaded your freebie. For those subscribers, you might have more selling points in the emails because you're still trying to convert them into buyers.

For the buyers, you might send private invitations to a special webinar you're hosting where they can interact with you and ask you questions – or hear an interview you're doing with another expert.

Various Perks to Offer Your List

There's a saying online about having a subscriber list. "Treat your list like gold." People like to say that the "money's in the list," and they're right.

Research shows it takes more than one visit from a person to convert into a buyer of your products and services. Once you have them on an email list, you have the ability to reach out to them and build trust with them.

So you always want to be thinking about the added value you can deliver. Here are a few ideas to get you started:

Free reports (again, you could write them yourself, hire a ghostwriter, or use PLR) that the public doesn't have access to:

- VIP access to something you created that isn't listed for the general public

- Discount codes for your list – so if the public pays $27 for a course you created, your list uses a code that saves them $10
- Advanced notice to access a course, product or service before the general public
- Additional bonus items that others won't have access to – because they aren't on the list

You want them to feel special being on your list – protected from bad information, and nurtured as a customer or follower of yours. Not only will this ensure they stay with you for a long time, but it helps them feel confident telling others about you as well.

Ways to Build Your List

There are many ways to build your list – some above the board, and some that border on spam tactics. You don't want to jeopardize your reputation by engaging in shady practices.

Giveaways are something you might want to consider. You can find other online professionals who have a website and list and create a page where each of you gives something away to those who sign up for their list.

Then each of you emails your list to inform them about the giveaway page. Everyone's subscribers go to the page and sign up for the free gifts they want, so now they're on more than one expert's list.

The best way to make this work is to really create an incredible value-based gift. Make it something that people will be amazed that you just shared for free. Many experts will give the least amount possible, but that's the opposite of what builds good will and trust with your customers.

Cross promotions are an option for you, too. You can partner with another expert who has a similar sized list and each agree to send out an email on behalf of the other with a message about them and a link to a free gift they can opt-in to.

Make sure you have an opt-in box in all the right places. You absolutely want to have one on your home page (and most of the other pages on your site as well). You also want one at the top of your blog in the sidebar.

Another good spot to place an opt-in box is the area right below each blog post. When someone lands on your blog and reads an entry, they often click out afterwards. But if they get to the end of the post and enjoyed it, that's the best time to give them the option to sign up and hear more!

Chapter 7

Master the Use of Multi Media

As someone who likes to share his or her expertise, you probably have a specific method that you like to deliver content to your audience, right?

Maybe you enjoy attending seminars and being a guest speaker, or writing books to showcase your talents.

Online, you're going to need to learn the fundamentals of several different media formats. It's not imperative that you use them all, but you're going to find that once you do expand your reach through a few styles, it increases the amount of people you can reach, drives more traffic to your website, and increases sales.

Not everyone learns and absorbs information in the same way. Some people do best when they have access to written words. Others are stimulated by visual sources, and some like to listen without distraction.

On the Internet, the media formats you choose will determine how big of a reach that you have. There are even specific websites that cater to those audiences – like how YouTube delivers video or Pinterest caters to graphic fans.

The best thing to do is start with the one you feel most confident with. If you're an expert who routinely attends seminars and gives speeches, then you might feel comfortable beginning with an online webinar using a service like GoToWebinar or WebinarJam.

If you're an author who wants to gain more fans for their writing online, then by all means, use text as a way to help you get your footing online.

But don't allow yourself to become so immersed in your comfort zone that you neglect the other wonderful possibilities available to you.

Text

Text is one of the only forms of media that's virtually a necessity. That's because the written word is what search engines use to figure out what your site is about. They "crawl" the words on your site and look for keywords and phrases that give them insight into how to index and rank your pages.

Keep your content relevant. Don't try to have a "one size fits all" website. It's best if it has a narrow focus – all related materials to bring in traffic. Make sure that when you write something, you organize your thoughts and don't ramble off on a tangent.

Don't worry about word count. You might start wondering things like, "How long should my blog post be?" or "How many pages should my eBook be?"

That's the wrong way to approach your online content. The correct answer is, "As long as it needs to be." You want to provide ample information so that you feel your message is complete.

Keep it conversational. You might have years of experience impressing college professors with your insight into whatever your niche is about. But an online audience responds differently to that type of writing.

Collegiate content is very academic – and you got rewarded for using that style. The Internet audience wants casual, conversational tones in the things they read. The rule of thumb is that you write content at an 8th grade level.

What you want to do is share information as if you were writing to a friend via email. This helps your audience feel more comfortable with you and it helps them digest the information better without having to look up terms and figure things out that might be above their head.

Use of text can include things like:

- Blog posts or static web pages
- EBooks (on your own site or Kindle)
- Viral reports
- Opt-in freebies
- Email autoresponders
- Social networking

So this is one area where you need to feel comfortable. If you don't think you're a good writer, then you might consider practicing the craft (because that improves your abilities), using a speech recognition tool like Dragon Naturally Speaking, or outsourcing an audio file to a transcription service.

Audio

Not everyone is into audio, but there are many people who love to listen to audio files on their MP3 while working out or in their car on the way to work or while working on other tasks at home or in the office. They're maximizing their time.

There are many resources that help you learn how to provide audio files to your audience. You'll need some basic tools that help you provide a good sound quality, like noise canceling headphones and a microphone.

You don't want a bunch of background noise diluting your message. Sometimes the distractions aren't anything we even notice – but our audience does. For example, you might think that because everyone's out of the house, it's quiet.

But your listener hears the loud whir of your air conditioner kicking on, or the swishy sound of your dishwasher running in the background. These are the noises you probably don't pay attention to, but they need to be filtered out of the audio file.

You also want to practice recording audio files and play them back and listen to them so that you see where you need to improve. For example, do you say, "Um..." too much? Are you coughing a lot or sipping coffee where the microphone picks it up?

Once you begin putting together podcasts that cater to your listening audience, you might branch out and offer written transcripts of the shows to your text-based audience. And then make a video series where you discuss the same thing for YouTube or Vimeo.

You can put your audio files on iTunes now and greatly increase your exposure. You might decide to charge for the content, or you might use it as a free method of building your brand and exposure to the right target audience.

Video

Use of video is one of the most popular media formats you can tackle right now. Some people don't want to put themselves out there – but until you feel comfortable putting yourself on camera, there are ways to use video and get around that requirement.

You can set up your camera to record a whiteboard where the video isn't aimed at you, but on your whiteboard where key concepts are being shared and your voice is guiding the experience.

You can use a tool like Camtasia and record a PowerPoint presentation on your computer. These tools can capture your screen at any size, do you might want to show different website or discuss something online as you talk and record the screen.

Setting is important when you're making a video. You want to project the right look for your video, but it doesn't mean you have to go so far as to invest in a green screen (but you can if you want to).

Instead, you basically want to reflect the right setting. If you were teaching knitting, then it would be perfectly find to record yourself sitting in a comfortable chair next to a lamp with your knitting materials around you.

If you're in a high financial business niche, then you might want to sit behind a luxurious looking desk in an office. Just try to match the topic to the look of your message.

Lighting has to be good in order for people to see the video. Some people record in dark rooms or have artificial lighting that gives off an eerie orange glow. You want to try using natural lighting whenever possible – but if you can't, work with your lighting to create something positive onscreen.

Sound quality has to be carefully monitored just like you do with audio. Make sure you get rid of background noise and that your own noises (like sipping drinks or clearing your through) aren't intrusive.

Length of the videos is different depending on what your purpose is. For most videos, shorter is better – 3-5 minutes is good. Going over 10 minutes cuts down on the number of people who will invest time in watching your video.

One good tip you can use is if you have a lengthy topic, just break the videos up into multiple parts. So if you're doing a 30-minute speech, you can break it up into three 10-minute videos or six 5-minute videos.

Tools you can use to create video are now less expensive. You can get small video cameras that hook right up to your computer. Or, you can even use a device like your iPhone to record a video and upload it to a site.

Places you can host your videos range from popular and free (like YouTube) to private and paid (like Vimeo Plus accounts). Or, you can upload the video straight to your website and host it there.

Do you want others to share them? Make sure the settings on your video are enabled to allow other people to share your video on their site. This can help increase your own traffic and sales.

Make sure you mention the name of your domain in the video so that people can stop by. So for example, if you're a life coach and you make a video that you'll allow other life coaches to share on their site, you might start out like this: "Hi, this is Jane Doe of JaneDoeCoaching.com, and I'm here to talk about..."

That way, even if the site owner doesn't credit you with a hyperlink to your site, the person watching the video will still learn about your domain name and be given the chance to visit it.

Infographics

Infographics are a type of media that is purely visual in nature, and they're spreading like wild fire. They're almost like unraveling a scroll with a wonderful message.

The reader starts at the top and learns something as they make their way down the image. There are words, images, statistics, and even hyperlinks they can follow online.

Infographics get shared on other people's sites, but they also find their way onto a newer and very trendy visual social network known as Pinterest.

Infographics work in any niche. Here are some examples of infographic ideas in various niches:

- How to Recycle
- 10 Ways to Get More Sleep
- 9 Healthy Smoothie Recipes
- How to Change Your Life Today

You can go to a stock photo site and gather some images that suit your niche and then create a visually pleasing info-board that shares insight with people in your target audience.

There are paid tools and free tools that help you build Infographics. There are also service providers who let you outsource the task to them. But they charge a lot of money, so if you're on a budget, you might want to learn on your own.

Don't try to do too much, too soon when it comes to utilizing multimedia formats. It's okay to take your time, but keep pushing yourself out of your comfort zone so that you make progress.

Chapter 8

Spread the Word on Social Networking Sites

Having a website online is a great anchor for your business where people can always find your expertise and your products. But it's not one of those situations where "if you build it, they will come."

You still have to go out and network online in a way that helps drive traffic to your site. Eventually, as you add more content to your blog, traffic will be pulled in via the search engines.

But social networking adds another layer of traffic generation. The best thing about it is that it's almost always free to use, popular with a lot of people, and readily available for you to use to share your message.

There are four major social networking strategies you'll want to pursue, but they're always evolving. Sometimes a certain platform becomes outdated, as the once popular MySpace did. So stay abreast of the trends and make sure you have a presence wherever possible.

Twitter

Twitter is a site where you can grow a large following in a relatively short amount of time just by following people who routinely talk about your niche topic – and other experts in the niche.

You want to create an account based around the branding you hope to do – whether it's for a business name (like "Holistic Health") or your own name. Accounts are free, and you can register more than one if you like, although that means more time has to be devoted to the site.

You're given a space where you can send out short "Tweets" of 140 characters (not words). You can Tweet hyperlinks that drive people to your site, but you'll want to include some text with that so they know what the link is about.

Start out by conducting a search and seeing who is discussing your niche topic. For example, let's say your passion is gardening and you've decided to take that online and profit from it.

You would conduct an initial search for the word *gardening*. When you type the word and get the results, you'll find accounts from others discussing it. For example, here are a few accounts that you could follow along with the number of followers they have at the time of this writing:

- @mthrearthlivin – Mother Earth Living – 5,424 followers
- @PermacultureMag – Permaculture Magazine – 10,674 followers
- @GardenerForFun – Gardener for Fun – 5,548 followers

All of those are accounts with a healthy amount of followers (some people have hundreds of thousands of followers). Some accounts only have 300 followers – but they might be extremely loyal and active on Twitter, so don't discount someone because of the size of their following.

You want to start following and interacting with others in your niche. This will get them to follow you back. When they're following you, they'll see the Tweets that you send out – and if they Re-Tweet (share) your Tweet with *their* followers, then it helps drive traffic to your site.

Facebook

Facebook has several ways you can cater to the people in your niche market and build a brand that gets followed. Some people go on Facebook and mistakenly start adding customers to their personal Facebook account.

You can keep those separate easily by creating a Facebook Fan Page or Group for your followers to join instead. A Fan Page is typically for a leader in a niche, so if you're branding yourself that way (which you should be – either as a business or person), then you can make a Fan Page to attract customers to.

A Facebook Group is slightly different and creates a more interactive element among users. You might want to use this to form a group of enthusiasts or like-minded people.

Another way people like to use Facebook in order to increase branding and profits is to use their paid advertising system. They let you run advertisements (where you can mix text and images) to a targeted group of people.

You can choose people based on geographic regions, age, gender, or interests. So if someone had gardening in their profile or had liked some gardening pages, you could promote your ad to them and expect a better conversion rate than if you promoted it to a broader group of people.

Facebook can generate some serious traffic to your site – but you have to put the time into developing your page. It's not about fancy graphics, but more about the personal interaction you do on the site with those who follow you.

You can also come up with some perks just for your followers on Facebook, like discounts or contests where they get rewarded for sharing your page or links with others.

Note: You can follow me on Facebook at:

Facebook.com/InternetIncomeCoach

Go ahead and like my page at the link above, I'd love to connect with you there.

Google Plus

Google created its very own social networking site – Google Plus. At first, people expected it to quickly put Facebook out of business. It didn't. It kind of sagged in popularity for a while.

But then it bounced back with a few tweaks and now it's booming. Men and women of all ages are joining and finding that they can separate their interests with what Google calls "Circles."

You could easily use this for both business and personal reasons, but let's look at it from a business perspective. Let's say you're a life coach who has many different types of clients – athletes, teenagers, women, etc.

You could have one large life coaching circle or individual circles that categorize the clients into one narrower group of individuals. Your messages could be private for each circle, or you could create public messages that go out to all of your circles.

Google Plus also has what's known as Events that you can set up to attract a wider audience. For example, you might be hosting a webinar and you want to announce it and have it where people can keep track of it online. The Events feature lets you do this.

You can create a Google Plus Page, too. Pages are very similar to your Google Plus profile, but there are some minor differences. With a page, you'll be able to have more administrators than just yourself, so if you want to collaborate with another person, you can.

Google also has Hangouts built into the system. This is a video chat with up to nine other individuals. So perhaps you want to start a group coaching session – Hangout with them at the specified time and record it so that you can share it with others who couldn't attend.

If you join, make sure you set up Google Authorship online through your Google Plus account. Authorship is a really neat way to boost your exposure online and get more clicks in the Google search engine.

If you conduct some searches on Google, once in a while you'll see someone's thumbnail picture right alongside their website hyperlink. This is a perk Google offers the G+ users if you set it up (which many don't know how to do).

The best thing about it is that when the search results come up with ten possibilities for someone, their eye is automatically drawn to the one with the image – your image – so you gain a better possibility that your link will be clicked on.

Note: You can follow me on Google Plus at:

InternetIncomeCoach.com/googleplus

Pinterest

Pinterest is a very visual website where people (primarily women, but some men belong to the site, too) go to "pin" their favorite things on their boards. Your goal in using Pinterest is to have your brand become one of those shared items.

The first thing you want to do is sign up for your free Pinterest account. You can use your name or business name, depending on how you want to be branded online.

Once there, you can create various boards. Before you start creating your own boards, you might want to conduct a search for a niche keyword and see how others are organizing their boards and pins.

For example, if your goal is to teach container gardening, then do a search for that and look at the boards people have. Here are some examples:

- Garden planters
- Best flowers for small spaces

- Everything tomatoes
- Herbs and spices
- Window gardening

You, of course, can categorize your own boards any way you like – this is just to help give you ideas of what fellow Pinterest users are doing because these are your prospective customers and clients.

If you have a blog, you're going to want to use images on the posts (at least one) so that you can Pin the post to Pinterest (it's a visual site). So let's say you create a blog post about how to grow tomatoes on the balcony.

You could either take a picture of your own creation, or go to a stock photo site like istockphoto.com and buy a small picture for about $1 that you can use on your blog.

Then you can go to Pinterest and upload the Pin (your blog URL) and it was find the image and pin it for you to one of your boards – with the image being hyperlinked back to your domain.

What happens then is that your prospective customers go onto Pinterest and conduct their own search about tomatoes. They see your Pin pop up. Not only do they "RePin" it to their own board, complete with your link intact, but they may choose to follow all of your boards for any future pins that you have.

The person who RePins your Pins is also exposing that to all of *their* followers. So if they have other friends who garden, then they can RePin your Pins and the blog post goes viral quickly.

Many businesses have taken up a Pinterest account and seen wonderful results. If you're in a niche like coaching and you're not sure what type of images to use, try something motivational like a quotation or a word.

For example, on istockphoto.com you could buy a $1 picture that says the words You Can Do It! That might accompany a blog post you do to inspire people t get past their hurdles.

Forums

While forums aren't exactly what are known as a social network, they're similar because it's where conversations and sharing take place. Sometimes, it's even better because the focus is narrower than on a major social network.

There are forums for just about any niche you can imagine. You can join one or more – or even start your own right on your site by installing a free forum or using a paid tool where you can keep the forum private and keep out spammers.

Forums are a wealth of information and opportunity. You can scroll through the posts and see what people want to know, just by looking at the thread titles – and then use those questions as the foundation for content that you put on your blog.

Or, you can jump in and start participating right on the forum and begin showcasing your expertise. Most forums allow you to have what's known as a "sig file," which stands for signature file.

This is a place where you can put a hyperlink to your blog or website. So if you're sharing really good information and helping people on the forums, you can rest assured they'll be clicking through to learn more on your own site.

Chapter 9

Producing & Promoting Your Own Products

If you're new to online marketing, you might be wondering how you can further the growth of your business by becoming a highly regarded global expert. While it might sound far-fetched – it's not. In fact, it's very easy to do!

Minisites

Minisites, where you sell your own info products, are going to be fantastic for you to use as a way to increase profits and branding online. A minisite is usually a one to five page site that includes:

- Sales letter
- Disclaimer page (which protects you legally against any claims)
- Affiliate page (to tell other marketers how they can promote you for a commission)
- Contact page

You basically have the framework for a sales page that promotes an eBook course that you've created. The sales letter has these elements on it:

- Headlines
- Sub-headlines
- Storyline
- Bullet points
- Testimonials

- Images (like before and after, progress, or proof shots)
- Order button
- Guarantee (if you want to offer one)
- Postscripts (because some people scroll all the way to the P.S. to have you sum it all up)

The process is simple. First, write an eBook about a topic you're passionate about. Once you complete it using a word processor, convert it into a PDF file.

Right click on the file and zip it up and place it into a secure area on your hosting account. Set up an automated delivery system so that if someone buys while you're sleeping, the system will process the order and deliver the product. A good tool for this is Download Guard.

While you're writing the course, have a graphic designer create your minisite design and then when it's delivered, set it up live on your website. You can either sell through PayPal directly or use sites like ClickBank to help you process orders.

You can create broad courses or narrow ones. You want to be considering how you can build your own little eBook empire online – because it helps position you as the go-to expert in your niche.

Membership Sites

Membership sites are a little more complex to launch, but they can really be a good source of consistent ongoing income once you get one going. People join memberships online so they can have some camaraderie with like-minded people and have access to information that's not available to the general public.

There is software that you can buy that will manage a membership site for you. When someone signs up, it will help them generate login details. It will process payments and even lock them out if they discontinue their membership.

The great thing about membership sites is that they generate a nice, steady income for you month after month – usually growing in size. You can expect a certain number of people to drop out, but the overall profits should grow.

The one thing you have to know you can do is handle the membership content load. Memberships typically are on-going, so you'll need to have a set schedule where you provide the content they're paying for.

There's another way that you can set up a membership, too. All you have to do is create a set amount of content that will be drip-fed to the member over time. So for example, you could create a 12-month course.

When the new member signs up, they're able to access each new month's worth of content after payment is process every 30 days. You can even get started with one month and start creating the rest as you go – as long as you're sure you'll have it by the deadline.

Video Courses

Video blogging is something that will help attract more loyal fans to your blog. But you can also put together video courses where you're teaching people whatever your niche is all about.

Screen capture tools will allow you to capture things on your PC screen. You can use this if you're teaching how to do something online, or you can record a PowerPoint.

Use a small video camera to record yourself talking or showing how to do something. Flip video used to be popular for this, but they went out of business, so you might look into a product like Kodak. These days most smartphones have high quality, HD cameras, built right into them.

Process the files and zip them up and then host them on your hosting account for the buyer to download to their computer. This prevents them from having to wait for the video to stream online (especially helpful for people who live in the middle of nowhere and have a slow Internet connection).

Others might prefer to watch it online, so you can host the files on your hosting account – or using a system like Amazon S3 (or Vimeo Pro) to host it for a small fee.

Videos add value to a course, so if you have an eBook course, like How to Knit a Baby Blanket, for example – you can also create a series of videos to go along with it that teach them how to do it from a visual standpoint.

Some people add the videos as a bonus, while others make them a standalone product or an upgrade in the purchase.

Consulting

Consulting or coaching is something you can do in many niches. People are looking for advice – and you can give them that in the form of an eBook, audio course or video files.

But they also want some one-on-one handholding from time to time. This is especially beneficial for niches like life coaches, dieting, and relationships. You can set up a service that you offer where the customer "meets" with you via Skype for a certain amount of time – like 30 minutes.

Mentoring like this can range anywhere from $100 per half hour to thousands. You can set up recurring coaching with some clients, or offer one-time meetings with you.

Note: if you'd like to learn more about the lucrative coaching and consulting niche I recommend checking out my book ***Coaching and Consulting Made Easy***.

Kindle

Kindle is a branch of online business that helps boost your authority in a niche. It's a global platform on Amazon where you can self-publish for free and get exposure in many different countries.

Kindle is similar to publishing an eBook on a minisite – but it eliminates the need for a website completely. The only difference is price points. On a minisite, you can easily charge $27-97 for an eBook course.

On Kindle, the average price is anywhere from $0.99 to $9.99. Usually, most Kindle authors price their books at $2.99 and use them as a lead to get more people to their websites.

Inside your Kindle eBook, you can place a link to your domain where you can capture the reader's name and email address. Or, you can hyperlink to your Facebook Fan Page or other social networking accounts.

One thing that many professionals do is create an introductory Kindle book and price it at $0.99. That gets as many buyers into your grasp as possible. Then the follow up books (which are promoted in the back of each book) are priced a bit higher and each one helps you gain more exposure in your niche.

Making a Kindle book is very easy. You can write it in a word processor and then save it as an HTML file before uploading it to Kindle. It's best to have a professional eCover created for your Kindle book – they cost around $47 to have made for you.

Kindle is going to give you an option of letting you enroll in the KDP Select plan. This restricts you from selling the eBook elsewhere, but it gives you the ability to give you book away for five out of the 90 days you're enrolled in it.

It also lets Kindle users check your book out of the lending library if they're members of the Prime feature on Amazon. You get paid (sometimes more than what you've priced the book for), and more prospective clients and customers get introduced to you.

Chapter 10

Adding Multiple Streams of Internet Income

Your passion and expertise for a subject is what will build trust and loyalty with your audience. You'll be blogging and creating content to share. You might also be offering coaching or mentoring to your global online customers.

But there's another very common method that experts online use to boost their profits by an incredible amount. It's called affiliate marketing, and it integrates seamlessly into your existing strategy.

Affiliate marketing is perfect for experts because you're already striving to be a leader and guide in your niche. Let's say you wanted to promote yourself as a sleep expert to your audience. Or a counselor who helps with insomnia.

If your client asked you which pillow you recommend, you'd tell them your personal preferences – or give them an answer for what you think might work best for them, right?

When you make that recommendation, you can get paid for it as an affiliate, earning a commission on your recommended resources for your audience.

How to Add on to Your Profits

In chapter 2 we touched on a scenario where affiliate marketing could help you make a different kind of profit. To fully understand it, we have to expand on the concept and teach you some best practices.

Any time you're sharing information about a niche, you can look for opportunities to add on an affiliate income stream. We're going to go through some scenarios, but the key to making this work is in taking your existing message and looking for ways you can supplement it with product advice.

There are millions of products out there that offer an affiliate program. While we're talking about this, it's important to point out that your own products can be enrolled in an affiliate program too – and you can have an army of affiliates out on the Internet promoting for you, helping increase your own income without effort on your part.

Typically, affiliate programs offer approximately 50% of the sale as commission. You might initially balk at that, thinking it sounds too high when you're the product creator – but the amount of sales affiliates can drive to your site is incredible – and you do nothing to pay for the traffic they generate, which takes a lot of effort.

Different Types of Affiliate Links

Affiliate products can be promoted on your blog, in your email autoresponders, on social networking sites, within your eBooks and more. There are two types of links you can use – text and image-based.

A text hyperlink is a link where the words you write are live links to the product. So you might be writing about the best knitting needle, and hyperlink those three words – best knitting needle.

You'll use a special link that includes your affiliate ID code in it. The program will help you generate it. For example, if you're an affiliate for Amazon.com, then you would go to the page you want to promote and click the Link To This Page tab at the top.

That will automatically help you create a link with your Amazon Associates ID embedded into it. Whenever someone buys through that link, you'll see it the following day in your reports – and you'll earn a commission that will be paid to you in 2 months.

Then there are the image-based affiliate links. This can be done a couple of ways. You can hyperlink a picture on your blog, so that if the reader clicks on the image, you get credit for the sale if they buy.

Or, you can grab pre-made banner ads that affiliate programs offer to you. Amazon has these, but so do product owners who let you promote their digital courses.

Some consumers have what's known as banner blindness, meaning they ignore graphics on a website. But it might work for some niches. You just don't want your blog to get bogged down in banners and buttons. Use them sparingly and strategically and test the results to see if you're making any sales.

Where to Sign Up to Promote as an Affiliate

You're going to want to promote a mix of digital and tangible products whenever possible. Digital products would be text and video courses that compete with or complement your own courses.

There's nothing wrong with promoting a competing niche marketer. Consumers often buy multiple resources when they want to learn a skill or find a solution. You can double your profits using this strategy – and it shows you're not intimidated by the competition.

For digital courses, you can go to a site like ClickBank.com, where you'll find info courses in a wide variety of niches, including:

- Relationships
- Diet and fitness
- Skincare
- Gardening
- Pets
- ...and more

So let's say you're the author of a book about preventing divorce. You can promote other people's "relationship saving" courses, too – especially if they have different tips than yours does.

Or perhaps you have a service or product business of your own, like organic skincare. You could promote a digital ecourse about this very topic and get paid 50% or more of a product priced anywhere from $27 to $97 or more.

Aside from ClickBank, you can also promote info product on Amazon Kindle, but the price points are low, so commission will be, too. Still, it adds up over time with volume of sales.

Now on the tangible side, you always want to be looking at what you can add onto your message. Let's say you were a motivational coach who helped people overcome depression.

One of your blog posts might be about Seasonal Affective Disorder – where people suffer from depression due to a lack of good lighting during the winter months.

You could go onto Amazon.com and grab an affiliate link for a sun therapy lamp – the kind where they plug it in and absorb quality light for about 30 minutes. These sell for over $100, and you could make about $7 per sale.

But Amazon isn't the only place that has tangible items to promote. There are many websites online with physical products and you can find them through sites like Commission Junction, Linkshare and Share a Sale.

If you know of a product that you want to promote, scroll to the bottom of the website and look to see if they have an affiliate program. Many will advertise it right on the page for you so that you can sign up and promote instantly.

Or, you can go to Google and search for your niche and the words "affiliate program." For example, you can go to Google and type in "gardening affiliate program" and get these kinds of results:

- Gardener's Supply Company – pays 9% of all sales
- Garden.com – pays 9-13% of online orders
- Freeplants.com – pays 75% plus bonuses
- DirectGardening.com – pays a flat rate $6 on each order

So you can sign up for a myriad of programs and see which ones convert better for you as you share your own expertise online with your audience.

Finding Good Products to Promote

You always want to remember that any time you recommend something to your audience, they're relying on you to steer them in the right direction. You'll be putting your own reputation at risk if you become an affiliate for shoddy products, even if you weren't the product creator.

The key to good conversions and profits – and to boosting your brand in your niche – is in knowing how to pick the right products to promote. There are some simple tactics you can use to ensure you're choosing only the best items available.

Keep the products relevant to your audience.

The top thing you want to keep in mind is that you're shopping for the needs of your audience. If they're into healthy nutrition, don't promote a homemade ice cream maker.

If they want to learn meditation, don't promote survival gear to them – the two topics need to be closely related. Meditation and yoga would be a good match, for example.

Know their average price point.

As you become a leader online in your niche, you're going to know approximately what your audience will spend. You'll get an idea of what that price point is based on what converts for you.

If you're promoting $27 items and they sell great, but $97 items won't move, then you know which works better and you can choose items to promote as an affiliate that are in the same price range.

Research the creator of the product to determine their ethics.

If it's a digital product, like another eBook or video course, find out who the product owner is and do a little digging on Google to see what kind of reputation they have.

You want to avoid anyone who has a reputation for being spammy to their buyers. When you recommend a product, you're telling your audience that this product – as well as its creator – are above the board.

Buy or get a copy of the product yourself.

Many product creators of digital products will be happy to send you what's known as a review copy. If you approach them, tell them about your own expertise and give them a link to your site.

Let them know that you'd like to possibly do a review of their product to promote it to your subscribers. Most of the time they'll set you up with instant access – and even provide some tools to help you promote the product.

If you feel like you'd be pressured to only write positive things if the product creator gave you access, then spend some money and buy it for yourself to review.

Even tangible products often have sample or trial offers. You can contact a manufacturer to find out if they would be willing to send you samples that you could test for a review on your blog.

Whether it's an online digital course or a tangible offline product, make sure you see what consumers are saying about it. Amazon has star ratings and customers give thoroughly reviews on items they buy.

If it's a digital online course, you really can't go by sales page testimonials because that doesn't give you a clear picture of the truth. Instead, look online in forums to see if anyone has started a discussion about it. If not, feel free to start one yourself and get feedback.

The Best Way to Review a Product for Profits

Start with telling your audience why you decided to review a particular product. Was it because several subscribers have asked about a solution and this seems like a viable one?

Take them through the buying process – this is especially important if you're buying online. What did the commercial (for tangibles) or sales copy (for digital) promise to the consumer? Did you get the course instantly, or have to wait? Were you bombarded by other offers as you tried to check out?

When you actually go through the review process, if it's possible, implement the steps as the product owner teaches you. If it's a tangible product, make sure you follow directions carefully.

If it's an ecourse, don't give away all of the product creator's tips and secrets – that would not only be unethical, but it would hinder your ability to convert the reader into a buyer.

Instead, just say something like this, "He shows me how to get instant relief from a headache and the next time I had one, I tried it. It took 2 minutes, but the headache was gone for good."

In that example, you're sharing the fact that you implemented a strategy, but you're not divulging someone else's secrets.

Make sure you're honest about everything – your likes and dislikes, things that worked versus things that didn't. You'll gain more of a stellar reputation if you protect your subscribers like they were family.

This also helps your entire conversion rate increase. If they know over time that you're truthful with them about what's good and what's not, then when you DO find something great, they'll buy without hesitation.

In the end, give your overall recommendation about the product – and whether or not you think it's a good buy for them. If it's only good for some people, then expand on that.

Affiliate marketing isn't for everyone. You might prefer to go forward with your online branding and business without promoting anyone else's products or services, and that's okay, too. You just need to be aware of all of your options when it comes to profiting online, and affiliate marketing is a big strategy for many people.

Don't wait until everything's perfect or you feel like you're "good enough" to start marketing online. Everything is tweakable on the Internet. You can change it with ease.

There's an audience out there right now who is hoping to find someone with your exact message, delivered in the way that only you can deliver it. Every moment you put it off is a missed opportunity to help someone find a solution they need to make life better.

Recommended Resources

The following are my recommended resources at the time of publishing. You can always access my most up-to-date recommended resources at:

InternetIncomeCoach.com/resources

Wordpress: I recommend building your website / blog using the Wordpress platform. Most good web hosting companies will allow you to install Wordpress free on your hosting account.

NameCheap: When it comes to domain names, most people are familiar with GoDaddy. For reasons I won't get into here, I personally use and recommend NameCheap to buy my domain names. You can learn more about NameCheap at:

InternetIncomeCoach.com/namecheap

HostGator: For hosting your website and blog, I recommend using HostGator. As mentioned above; you can install the Wordpress platform free on a HostGator hosting account. Use coupon code "incomecoach25" at HostGator.com to save 25% off your order of any new hosting account. You can learn more about HostGator at:

InternetIncomeCoach.com/hostgator

GoToWebinar: For doing live video presentations and training (webinars) my favorite tool is GoToWebinar by Citrix. You can read my review of GoToWebinar and get a 30 day free trial at:

InternetIncomeCoach.com/gtw

WishList Member: If you are interested in creating an online membership program, I highly recommend using WishList Memember, which integrates with your Wordpress site to give it membership functionality. You can learn more about WishList Member at:

InternetIncomeCoach.com/wishlistmember

About the Author

Brian T. Edmondson is an author, speaker, and Internet entrepreneur who helps website owners get more website traffic, build their email lists, and increase sales online.

After leaving his "Wall Street" job in 2001, Brian found true success and independence through the power of the Internet. He has launched several websites, including one that grossed over $50,000 in sales in the first week and has masterminded many multi-million dollar Internet businesses.

Brian has worked and consulted with many of the world's top online companies and entrepreneurs including Agora Publishing, Early to Rise, American Writer's & Artists, Michael Masterson and MaryEllen Tribby, just to name a few. He is also the co-author of The Ultimate Success Secret with Dan Kennedy.

He truly lives "the internet lifestyle", working full time online from his home outside of Philadelphia, PA (or anywhere he can get his MacBook Air connected to the internet).

You can learn more about Brian and download a free copy of his most up-to-date publication, ***The Internet Profit Report***, at **InternetIncomeCoach.com**.

More From This Author

Coaching and Consulting Made Easy: *How to Start, Build, and Grow A Profit Pulling Coaching Business by Turning Your Knowledge Into Money*

Blogging for Coaches & Consultants Made Easy: *How to Get More Traffic, Build Your Platform, and Attract More Clients with a Powerful Business Blog*

The Ultimate Success Secret: *Is It Possible That There Is One Single, Super-Powerful Secret of Success of Far Greater Importance Than All Others? with Dan S. Kennedy, Michael M. Capuzzi, et al*

One Last Thing...

I truly hope that you received a ton of value from this book and enjoyed reading it as much as I enjoyed writing it.

If you did, I'd be extremely grateful if you could take just 30 seconds to leave a good rating, a positive review, and share this book with your friends on social media.

It would mean a lot to me; and help others discover this great opportunity and journey which you just completed and are about to embark on.

Thank you again, and I hope that our paths cross again in the near future.

To your internet marketing success!

- Brian

Made in the USA
Monee, IL
08 November 2026

67971472R00094